P9-BYD-778

FORTY-FIVE

cloverleaf books™

Community Helpers

Let's Meet a Teacher

Bridget Heos

illustrated by **Kyle Poling**

M MILLBROOK PRESS · MINNEAPOLIS

With thanks to fourth-grade teacher
Kelly Crawford Van Maren —B.H.

For my teachers throughout the
years at Circleville City Schools and
Columbus College of Art & Design —K.P.

Text and illustrations copyright © 2013 by Lerner Publishing
Group, Inc.

Millbrook Press
A division of Lerner Publishing Group, Inc.
241 First Avenue North
Minneapolis, MN 55401 U.S.A.

Website address: www.lernerbooks.com

Main body text set in Slappy Inline 18/28.
Typeface provided by T26.

Library of Congress Cataloging-in-Publication Data

Heos, Bridget.
    Let's meet a teacher / by Bridget Heos ; illustrated by Kyle
Poling.
       p.   cm. — (Cloverleaf books—community helpers)
    Includes index.
    ISBN 978–0–7613–9026–8 (lib. bdg. : alk. paper)
    1. Teachers—Juvenile literature. I. Poling, Kyle. II. Title.
LB1775.H453 2013
371.1—dc23   2012022481

Manufactured in the United States of America
1 – BP – 12/31/12

TABLE OF CONTENTS

Chapter One
Lots of Learning

Our class is on a mission. We want to find out what a **teacher** does. We decide to visit Ms. Crawford. She teaches the fourth grade.

"I'm a learning expert," says Ms. Crawford.
"What does that mean?" asks Noah.
"Come inside my classroom. I'll show you."

"Today my class is learning about animal homes," says Ms. Crawford. Her classroom is so **quiet**. Everyone is busy reading and writing.

6

Molly raises her hand. "Why aren't you teaching?"

"I am," Ms. Crawford says. "I'm teaching them how to learn by reading. But reading time is done now."

In elementary school, classroom teachers teach most subjects. They often teach math, English, social studies, and science. In middle school and high school, most teachers teach one subject.

Ms. Crawford says there are many ways to learn. Today she is teaching the students to **learn from one another.**

They put their animal notes on a **whiteboard** that connects to a computer. Everyone takes turns being a teacher.

RULES

Teachers have many classroom tools. They use chalk and markers on chalkboards and whiteboards. Other whiteboards work with a computer. Teachers also have classroom supplies such as pens, pencils, and worksheets. And of course, they have lots of books!

Chapter Two

Stickers and Red Pens

Who taught Ms. Crawford to teach?
Ms. Crawford says she learned to
be a teacher in **college**.

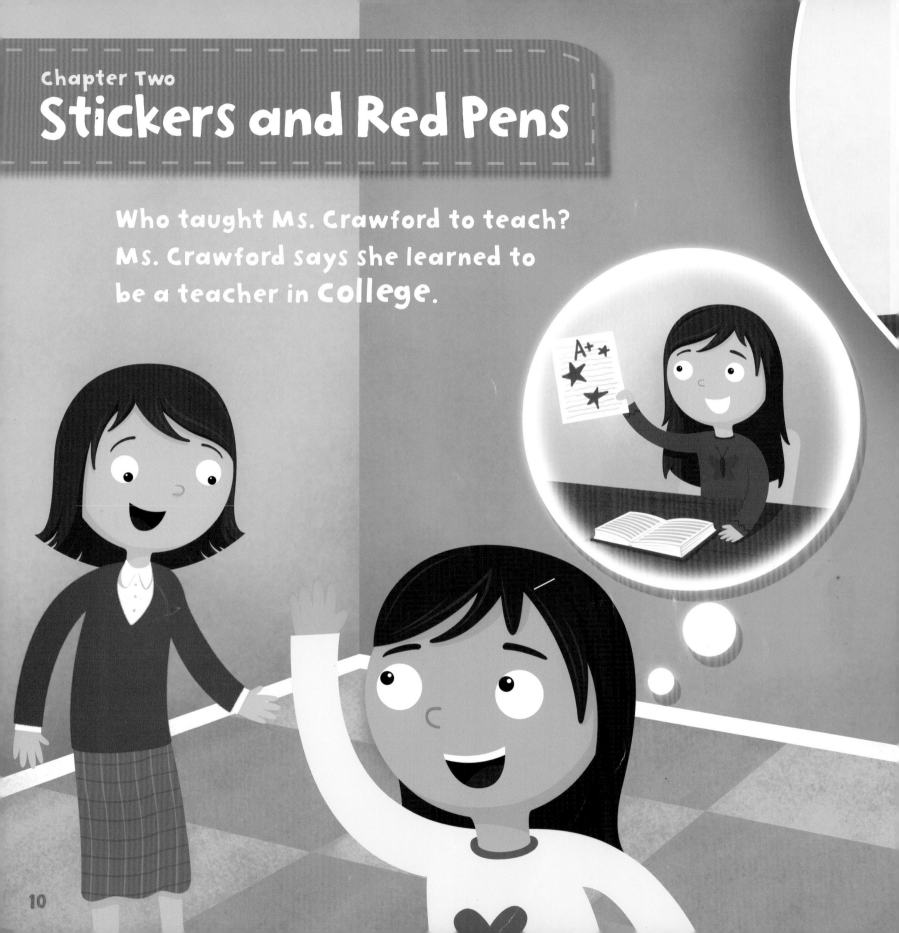

"I bet you got stars on all your work." Bella says.

Ms. Crawford smiles. "I worked my hardest. That's what I want my students to do too."

People learning to be teachers are called student teachers. They watch other teachers teach. Then they practice teaching a class themselves.

"One of my jobs is to check my students' work," says Ms. Crawford.

She shows us a sheet of homework. She put a **sticker at the top.**

Teachers are workers in the community. A community is a group of people who live in the same city, town, or neighborhood.

"I can tell this student **worked hard**,"
Ms. Crawford says. "She did her best."

Edward raises his hand. "Don't you want your students to make mistakes? Then you get to use your **red pen**."

Ms. Crawford laughs. "No, I want them to get the answers right. That shows me they have learned. It shows that I did a good job teaching."

Teachers never stop learning. They take special classes to learn how to be even better at what they do. They also go to large meetings called conferences. There they share ideas about teaching with other teachers.

Chapter Three

Paper Clips and Pizza Parties

Making **classroom rules** is another part of a teacher's job. Rules teach students how to be good community members.

RULES
FOR MS. CRAWFORD'S CLASS

★ Be respectful and responsible.

★ Pay attention and follow directions.

★ Raise your hand to speak.

★ Keep hands and feet to yourself.

★ Be prepared for class and ready to learn!

Ms. Crawford's rules help her students be kind and work hard.

Teachers and schools have been around a long time. The first public school in America opened in 1635. It is in Boston. Some of our country's earliest leaders went there. The school is still open but is now in a different building.

"What are these?" asks Jorge. He points to a chain of paper clips.

Teachers who teach the same grade share ideas. Their classes may also work on projects together. Sometimes they celebrate following rules together too.

"They are **rewards**," Ms. Crawford says. "The class gets a paper clip for following our classroom rules. When the chain reaches the floor, we have a pizza party. The other fourth-grade class has paper clips too."

Ms. Crawford **rings a bell.** It's time for a math lesson. It's also time for our class to go back to our room.

We're excited for fourth grade. Ms. Crawford lends her students a helping hand. So we give her a hand. Hooray for Ms. Crawford!

Make a Pencil Holder

Most teachers have a lot of pencils, pens, and markers. A pencil holder helps keep those important tools organized. Want to surprise *your* teacher with a homemade pencil holder? Here's how:

What you need:

an empty jar without the top · glue
yarn—1 or more colors · a paper plate
scissors · a paintbrush

1) Clean the outside of the jar. Take off any loose labels. Don't worry if some glue or paper is stuck to the jar. It will be covered with yarn.

2) Squeeze some glue onto a paper plate. Dip a paintbrush into the glue. Paint the outside of the jar, starting just below the rim. Stop after you've painted about one-fourth of the jar.

3) Starting at the top, wrap a piece of yarn around the jar. You can put your fingers inside the jar to turn it as you go. Continue to wrap the yarn around the jar until all the glue is covered. Try to keep the rows of yarn tight to one another. Cut the yarn where you finish.

4) Repeat steps 2 and 3, working your way down the jar. If you want to, you can change the colors of yarn as you go. Avoid putting glue or yarn on the bottom of the jar.

5) Set the jar someplace where the glue can dry for a day.

6) Bring it to school and give it to your teacher!

GLOSSARY

celebrate: to do something special to show that a day is important

college: a school that students go to after they finish high school

community: a group of people who live in the same area

conferences: large meetings where people gather to share ideas

expert: a person who knows a lot about something, such as teaching

notes: writings about what a person read, learned, saw, or heard

rewards: prizes earned for following rules and being a good community member

student teacher: a college student who is learning to be a teacher. A student teacher practices teaching in a classroom with another teacher's help.

subject: an area of learning, such as math or science

BOOKS

Bowen, Anne. ***What Do Teachers Do (After You Leave School)?*** Minneapolis: Carolrhoda, 2006.
In this funny picture book, see how teachers have fun when the school day ends.

Gall, Chris. ***Substitute Creacher.*** New York: Little, Brown, 2011.
The students in this story get an unusual teacher when their own teacher is away.

Green, Rhonda Gowler. ***This Is the Teacher***. New York: Puffin, 2006.
This funny story shows a teacher on the job.

Leake, Diyan. ***Teachers***. Chicago: Heinemann-Raintree, 2008.
Learn more about teachers in this book.

WEBSITES

Fun Jobs (Grades K–5)
http://www.kids.gov/k_5/k_5_careers.shtml
Find out about many different careers at this website.

I Believe In Me
http://www.ibelieveinme.org/GradesK_3.asp
This kid-friendly website includes information and activities about careers.

LERNER *e* **SOURCE**™
Expand learning beyond the printed book. Download free, complementary educational resources for this book from our website, www.lerneresource.com.